# 50 Morning Bliss: 50 Breakfast Recipes to Start Your Day Right

By: Kelly Johnson

# Table of Contents

- Classic Pancakes
- Fluffy Belgian Waffles
- Overnight Oats with Berries
- Spinach and Feta Omelette
- Avocado Toast with Poached Egg
- Banana Nut Muffins
- Greek Yogurt Parfait
- Breakfast Burrito
- French Toast with Maple Syrup
- Chia Seed Pudding
- Breakfast Quiche Lorraine
- Smoked Salmon Bagel
- Sweet Potato Hash
- Granola with Almond Milk
- Eggs Benedict
- Peanut Butter and Banana Smoothie
- Cinnamon Roll Pancakes
- Huevos Rancheros
- Veggie Breakfast Scramble
- Blueberry Scones
- Breakfast Tacos
- Protein-Packed Smoothie Bowl
- Classic English Breakfast
- Mushroom and Cheese Frittata
- Apple Cinnamon Overnight Oats
- Breakfast Croissant Sandwich
- Sweet Cornmeal Porridge
- Ricotta and Honey Toast
- Vegan Tofu Scramble
- Breakfast Pizza
- Raspberry Almond Danish
- Ham and Cheese Breakfast Casserole
- Chocolate Chip Banana Bread
- Savory Crepes with Spinach
- Maple Bacon Donuts

- Acai Smoothie Bowl
- Cottage Cheese with Fresh Fruit
- Breakfast Sausage and Egg Muffins
- Tropical Fruit Salad
- Pumpkin Spice Waffles
- Zucchini Bread
- Breakfast Nachos
- Mango and Coconut Chia Pudding
- Baked Oatmeal Bars
- Strawberry Yogurt Popsicles
- Breakfast Quesadilla
- Sourdough Toast with Ricotta and Berries
- Almond Butter and Jelly Overnight Oats
- Pear and Walnut Muffins
- Classic Breakfast Sandwich

## Classic Pancakes

**Ingredients:**

- 1 ½ cups (190g) all-purpose flour
- 3 ½ teaspoons baking powder
- 1 teaspoon salt
- 1 tablespoon granulated sugar
- 1 ¼ cups (300ml) milk
- 1 egg
- 3 tablespoons (45g) melted butter or vegetable oil

**Instructions:**

1. **Mix the dry ingredients:**
   In a large bowl, whisk together the flour, baking powder, salt, and sugar.
2. **Combine wet ingredients:**
   In a separate bowl, beat the egg, then whisk in the milk and melted butter (or oil).
3. **Make the batter:**
   Gradually pour the wet ingredients into the dry ingredients. Mix until just combined. The batter will be slightly lumpy, which is fine—overmixing can make the pancakes tough.
4. **Preheat the pan:**
   Heat a non-stick skillet or griddle over medium heat. Lightly grease it with butter or oil.
5. **Cook the pancakes:**
   Scoop ¼ cup of batter onto the skillet for each pancake. Cook until bubbles form on the surface and the edges look set, about 2-3 minutes. Flip and cook the other side for another 1-2 minutes, until golden brown.
6. **Serve warm:**
   Stack the pancakes and serve with your favorite toppings, such as maple syrup, butter, fresh fruit, or whipped cream.

**Fluffy Belgian Waffles**

**Ingredients:**

- 2 cups all-purpose flour
- 2 tablespoons sugar
- 1 tablespoon baking powder
- ¼ teaspoon salt
- 2 large eggs, separated
- 1 ¾ cups milk
- ½ cup vegetable oil
- 1 teaspoon vanilla extract
- 1 teaspoon almond extract (optional)
- ¼ teaspoon cream of tartar (for egg whites)

**Instructions:**

1. **Preheat the waffle iron:**
   Preheat your Belgian waffle iron according to the manufacturer's instructions.
2. **Mix the dry ingredients:**
   In a large bowl, whisk together the flour, sugar, baking powder, and salt.
3. **Combine the wet ingredients:**
   In a separate bowl, whisk the egg yolks, milk, vegetable oil, and vanilla extract (and almond extract, if using).
4. **Beat the egg whites:**
   In another clean bowl, beat the egg whites with a hand mixer or stand mixer until soft peaks form. Add cream of tartar and continue beating until stiff peaks form.
5. **Make the batter:**
   Pour the wet ingredients into the dry ingredients and stir until just combined. Gently fold in the beaten egg whites to the batter, being careful not to deflate the mixture.
6. **Cook the waffles:**
   Lightly grease the waffle iron with non-stick spray or oil. Pour enough batter into the waffle iron to cover the surface. Close the waffle iron and cook until golden brown and crisp, usually about 3-5 minutes.
7. **Serve:**
   Serve the waffles warm with your favorite toppings like syrup, whipped cream, fresh fruit, or powdered sugar.

**Overnight Oats with Berries**

**Ingredients:**

- ½ cup rolled oats
- 1 tablespoon chia seeds (optional)
- 1 cup milk (dairy or plant-based)
- ½ teaspoon vanilla extract
- 1 tablespoon honey or maple syrup
- ½ cup mixed berries (strawberries, blueberries, raspberries)

**Instructions:**

In a mason jar or bowl, combine oats, chia seeds, milk, vanilla extract, and sweetener. Stir to combine, cover, and refrigerate overnight. In the morning, top with fresh berries and enjoy.

## Spinach and Feta Omelette

**Ingredients:**

- 2 large eggs
- ½ cup fresh spinach, chopped
- 2 tablespoons feta cheese, crumbled
- 1 tablespoon olive oil or butter
- Salt and pepper, to taste

**Instructions:**

Beat the eggs with a pinch of salt and pepper. Heat olive oil or butter in a pan over medium heat. Add spinach and sauté until wilted, about 1-2 minutes. Pour the beaten eggs over the spinach and cook until the eggs set. Sprinkle feta cheese on one side, fold the omelette, and serve warm.

**Avocado Toast with Poached Egg**

**Ingredients:**

- 1 ripe avocado
- 2 slices whole-grain bread
- 2 large eggs
- 1 tablespoon vinegar (for poaching)
- Salt and pepper, to taste
- Red pepper flakes (optional)

**Instructions:**

Toast the bread to your desired crispiness. Mash the avocado and spread it evenly on the toasted bread. Season with salt, pepper, and red pepper flakes. For the poached eggs: Bring a pot of water to a simmer and add vinegar. Crack the eggs into the water and cook for 3-4 minutes. Remove with a slotted spoon. Place the poached eggs on top of the avocado toast and serve immediately.

## Banana Nut Muffins

**Ingredients:**

- 1 ½ cups all-purpose flour
- 1 teaspoon baking powder
- ½ teaspoon baking soda
- ¼ teaspoon salt
- 1 teaspoon cinnamon
- 2 ripe bananas, mashed
- 1/3 cup melted butter
- 1/2 cup sugar
- 1 large egg
- 1 teaspoon vanilla extract
- ½ cup chopped walnuts or pecans (optional)

**Instructions:**

Preheat the oven to 350°F (175°C). Grease or line a muffin tin. In a bowl, whisk together the flour, baking powder, baking soda, salt, and cinnamon. In another bowl, mix mashed bananas, melted butter, sugar, egg, and vanilla. Stir the wet ingredients into the dry ingredients, then fold in the nuts. Divide the batter among the muffin cups and bake for 18-20 minutes, or until a toothpick comes out clean. Let the muffins cool before serving.

**Greek Yogurt Parfait**

**Ingredients:**

- 1 cup Greek yogurt
- ½ cup granola
- ½ cup mixed berries (strawberries, blueberries, raspberries)
- 1 tablespoon honey or maple syrup (optional)

**Instructions:**

Layer Greek yogurt, granola, and mixed berries in a glass or bowl. Drizzle with honey or maple syrup, if desired. Serve immediately for a fresh and healthy breakfast.

**Breakfast Burrito**

**Ingredients:**

- 2 large eggs
- 2 tortillas
- ¼ cup shredded cheese
- ¼ cup salsa
- ½ avocado, sliced
- 1 tablespoon olive oil
- Salt and pepper, to taste
- ¼ cup cooked breakfast sausage or bacon (optional)

**Instructions:**

Heat olive oil in a pan and scramble the eggs with salt and pepper. Warm the tortillas in a separate pan. Once the eggs are cooked, assemble the burrito by adding eggs, cheese, salsa, avocado, and optional sausage or bacon to the tortillas. Roll up the tortillas and serve immediately.

**French Toast with Maple Syrup**

**Ingredients:**

- 2 slices bread (preferably thick-cut)
- 2 large eggs
- ½ cup milk
- 1 teaspoon cinnamon
- 1 teaspoon vanilla extract
- 1 tablespoon butter
- Maple syrup for serving

**Instructions:**

Whisk eggs, milk, cinnamon, and vanilla together. Dip the bread slices into the mixture, coating both sides. Heat butter in a pan over medium heat. Cook the bread slices until golden brown on both sides. Serve with maple syrup.

**Chia Seed Pudding**

**Ingredients:**

- 3 tablespoons chia seeds
- 1 cup milk (dairy or plant-based)
- 1 teaspoon vanilla extract
- 1 tablespoon maple syrup (optional)
- Fresh fruit or granola for topping

**Instructions:**

Mix chia seeds, milk, vanilla, and maple syrup (if using) in a bowl or jar. Stir well, cover, and refrigerate for at least 4 hours or overnight. Top with fresh fruit or granola before serving.

**Breakfast Quiche Lorraine**

**Ingredients:**

- 1 pre-made pie crust
- 4 large eggs
- 1 cup heavy cream
- ½ cup cooked bacon, crumbled
- ½ cup shredded Swiss cheese
- 1/3 cup chopped onion
- Salt and pepper, to taste

**Instructions:**

Preheat oven to 375°F (190°C). Whisk eggs and cream together, then stir in bacon, Swiss cheese, onion, salt, and pepper. Pour the mixture into the pie crust and bake for 35-40 minutes, or until set and lightly golden. Let cool slightly before slicing and serving.

**Smoked Salmon Bagel**

**Ingredients:**

- 1 whole wheat or plain bagel, split
- 2 ounces smoked salmon
- 2 tablespoons cream cheese
- 1 tablespoon capers
- 1 tablespoon red onion, thinly sliced
- Fresh dill, for garnish

**Instructions:**

Toast the bagel halves. Spread cream cheese on each half, then top with smoked salmon, capers, red onion, and dill. Serve immediately.

**Sweet Potato Hash**

**Ingredients:**

- 2 medium sweet potatoes, peeled and diced
- 1 bell pepper, diced
- 1 small onion, diced
- 1 tablespoon olive oil
- 1 teaspoon paprika
- Salt and pepper, to taste
- 2 eggs (optional)

**Instructions:**

Heat olive oil in a skillet over medium heat. Add diced sweet potatoes and cook until tender, about 10-15 minutes. Add bell pepper, onion, paprika, salt, and pepper. Cook for an additional 5 minutes. If desired, fry eggs in a separate pan and serve on top of the hash.

## Granola with Almond Milk

**Ingredients:**

- 1 cup granola
- 1 cup almond milk
- Fresh fruit (optional)

**Instructions:**

Pour almond milk over granola and serve with fresh fruit if desired. Enjoy as a quick and easy breakfast.

**Eggs Benedict**

**Ingredients:**

- 2 English muffins, split and toasted
- 4 large eggs
- 4 slices Canadian bacon or ham
- 1 cup hollandaise sauce (store-bought or homemade)
- Fresh chives for garnish

**Instructions:**

Poach the eggs by simmering water with a splash of vinegar. Toast the English muffin halves and layer each with a slice of Canadian bacon. Place a poached egg on top, then spoon hollandaise sauce over the egg. Garnish with chives and serve immediately.

## Peanut Butter and Banana Smoothie

**Ingredients:**

- 1 ripe banana
- 1 tablespoon peanut butter
- 1 cup milk (dairy or plant-based)
- 1 tablespoon honey or maple syrup (optional)
- ½ cup Greek yogurt (optional for creaminess)
- Ice cubes (optional)

**Instructions:**

Place all ingredients into a blender and blend until smooth. Adjust the consistency by adding more milk or ice if needed. Serve immediately.

**Cinnamon Roll Pancakes**

**Ingredients:**

- 1 ½ cups all-purpose flour
- 2 tablespoons sugar
- 1 tablespoon baking powder
- 1 teaspoon cinnamon
- 1 ¼ cups milk
- 1 large egg
- 2 tablespoons melted butter
- 1 teaspoon vanilla extract
- For the swirl: 3 tablespoons brown sugar, 1 teaspoon cinnamon, 2 tablespoons melted butter
- Cream cheese icing (optional)

**Instructions:**

In a large bowl, whisk together flour, sugar, baking powder, cinnamon, milk, egg, butter, and vanilla until smooth. In a small bowl, mix brown sugar, cinnamon, and melted butter for the swirl. Heat a griddle or pan over medium heat and lightly grease. Pour pancake batter onto the griddle and swirl the cinnamon mixture over each pancake. Cook until bubbles form, then flip and cook until golden. Drizzle with cream cheese icing, if desired.

**Huevos Rancheros**

**Ingredients:**

- 2 corn tortillas
- 2 large eggs
- ½ cup refried beans
- ½ cup salsa
- 1 tablespoon olive oil
- 1 tablespoon chopped cilantro
- 1 tablespoon sour cream (optional)
- Salt and pepper, to taste

**Instructions:**

Heat the olive oil in a pan and lightly toast the corn tortillas on each side. In the same pan, cook the eggs to your liking (fried or poached). Heat the refried beans and salsa in a small pot. Assemble the dish by layering the tortillas, beans, and salsa. Top with the eggs and garnish with cilantro and sour cream, if desired.

**Veggie Breakfast Scramble**

**Ingredients:**

- 3 large eggs
- 1 tablespoon olive oil or butter
- ½ cup bell peppers, diced
- ½ cup onions, diced
- ½ cup spinach, chopped
- ½ cup mushrooms, sliced
- Salt and pepper, to taste

**Instructions:**

Heat olive oil or butter in a skillet over medium heat. Add bell peppers, onions, and mushrooms and sauté until tender. Add spinach and cook until wilted. In a bowl, whisk eggs with salt and pepper, then pour them into the skillet. Stir constantly until eggs are scrambled and fully cooked. Serve warm.

**Blueberry Scones**

**Ingredients:**

- 2 cups all-purpose flour
- ¼ cup sugar
- 2 teaspoons baking powder
- ¼ teaspoon salt
- ½ cup cold butter, cubed
- 1 cup fresh blueberries
- 2/3 cup heavy cream
- 1 teaspoon vanilla extract
- 1 tablespoon milk (for brushing)

**Instructions:**

Preheat the oven to 375°F (190°C). In a bowl, whisk together flour, sugar, baking powder, and salt. Cut in the cold butter until the mixture resembles coarse crumbs. Gently fold in blueberries. Stir in heavy cream and vanilla until just combined. Drop spoonfuls of dough onto a baking sheet and brush with milk. Bake for 20-25 minutes or until golden brown.

## Breakfast Tacos

**Ingredients:**

- 4 small corn tortillas
- 2 large eggs
- ½ cup cooked breakfast sausage or bacon
- ½ cup shredded cheese
- ¼ cup salsa
- ¼ avocado, sliced
- Fresh cilantro for garnish

**Instructions:**

Warm the tortillas in a skillet. In a separate pan, scramble the eggs. Assemble each taco by placing eggs, sausage or bacon, cheese, salsa, and avocado on each tortilla. Garnish with cilantro and serve immediately.

**Protein-Packed Smoothie Bowl**

**Ingredients:**

- 1 banana, frozen
- 1 cup Greek yogurt
- 1 tablespoon almond butter or peanut butter
- 1 scoop protein powder (optional)
- 1 tablespoon chia seeds
- Toppings: granola, sliced fruit, nuts, seeds, or coconut flakes

**Instructions:**

Blend the frozen banana, Greek yogurt, almond or peanut butter, protein powder (if using), and chia seeds until smooth. Pour into a bowl and top with granola, sliced fruit, nuts, seeds, or coconut flakes.

## Classic English Breakfast

**Ingredients:**

- 2 sausages
- 2 slices bacon
- 1 tomato, halved
- 1 cup baked beans
- 2 eggs
- 2 slices toast
- Butter for toasting
- Salt and pepper, to taste

**Instructions:**

In a pan, cook the sausages and bacon until browned and cooked through. In the same pan, fry the tomato halves, cut-side down, until soft. Warm the baked beans in a pot. Toast the bread slices and butter them. In a separate pan, cook the eggs to your liking (fried or scrambled). Serve the eggs, sausages, bacon, beans, tomato, and toast together for a hearty English breakfast.

## Mushroom and Cheese Frittata

**Ingredients:**

- 6 large eggs
- 1 cup mushrooms, sliced
- 1/2 cup shredded cheese (cheddar, Swiss, or your choice)
- 1 small onion, diced
- 1 tablespoon olive oil
- Salt and pepper, to taste

**Instructions:**

Preheat the oven to 375°F (190°C). Heat olive oil in a skillet over medium heat and sauté onions and mushrooms until tender. In a bowl, whisk eggs with salt and pepper, then pour over the mushrooms. Sprinkle shredded cheese over the eggs and cook on the stovetop for 3-4 minutes. Transfer the skillet to the oven and bake for 10-15 minutes, or until the eggs are set. Slice and serve warm.

## Apple Cinnamon Overnight Oats

**Ingredients:**

- ½ cup rolled oats
- 1 cup almond milk (or any milk of your choice)
- 1 apple, diced
- 1 teaspoon cinnamon
- 1 tablespoon chia seeds (optional)
- 1 tablespoon maple syrup or honey
- A pinch of salt

**Instructions:**

In a jar or bowl, combine the oats, milk, diced apple, cinnamon, chia seeds (if using), maple syrup, and a pinch of salt. Stir well to combine. Cover and refrigerate overnight. In the morning, give it a good stir and enjoy!

**Breakfast Croissant Sandwich**

**Ingredients:**

- 1 croissant, halved
- 2 large eggs
- 1 slice cheese (cheddar, Swiss, or your choice)
- 2 slices cooked bacon or sausage patty
- 1 tablespoon butter
- Salt and pepper, to taste

**Instructions:**

In a skillet, melt butter over medium heat. Crack the eggs into the skillet and cook to your desired doneness (fried, scrambled, or poached). Season with salt and pepper. Toast the croissant halves. Assemble the sandwich by layering the cooked eggs, cheese, and bacon or sausage between the croissant halves. Serve immediately.

## Sweet Cornmeal Porridge

**Ingredients:**

- 1 cup cornmeal
- 3 cups water or milk (for creaminess)
- 1 tablespoon brown sugar or maple syrup
- 1 teaspoon vanilla extract
- Pinch of salt
- Cinnamon (optional)

**Instructions:**

In a saucepan, bring the water or milk to a boil. Slowly whisk in the cornmeal and reduce the heat to low. Cook, stirring frequently, until thickened (about 5-10 minutes). Stir in brown sugar, vanilla extract, and a pinch of salt. Sprinkle with cinnamon, if desired. Serve hot.

## Ricotta and Honey Toast

**Ingredients:**

- 2 slices of bread (sourdough or your choice)
- ½ cup ricotta cheese
- 1 tablespoon honey
- A sprinkle of cinnamon (optional)
- Fresh fruit for topping (optional)

**Instructions:**

Toast the bread slices to your desired crispness. Spread ricotta cheese generously on each slice. Drizzle with honey and sprinkle with cinnamon if using. Top with fresh fruit, such as berries or sliced figs, and serve immediately.

**Vegan Tofu Scramble**

**Ingredients:**

- 1 block firm tofu, drained and crumbled
- 1 tablespoon olive oil
- ¼ cup onion, diced
- ½ cup bell pepper, diced
- ¼ cup spinach, chopped
- 1 teaspoon turmeric
- 1 teaspoon garlic powder
- Salt and pepper, to taste
- Fresh herbs (optional)

**Instructions:**

Heat olive oil in a skillet over medium heat. Add the onions and bell peppers, and sauté until softened. Add the crumbled tofu, turmeric, garlic powder, salt, and pepper. Cook, stirring occasionally, for 5-7 minutes until tofu is heated through and slightly crispy. Stir in the spinach and cook until wilted. Garnish with fresh herbs, if desired, and serve hot.

**Breakfast Pizza**

**Ingredients:**

- 1 pizza crust (store-bought or homemade)
- 2 large eggs
- ½ cup mozzarella cheese, shredded
- ¼ cup tomato sauce
- ¼ cup cooked breakfast sausage or bacon (optional)
- 1 tablespoon fresh basil, chopped
- Salt and pepper, to taste

**Instructions:**

Preheat the oven to 400°F (200°C). Roll out the pizza dough onto a baking sheet. Spread tomato sauce evenly over the crust. Sprinkle with mozzarella cheese, and add the cooked breakfast sausage or bacon (if using). Carefully crack two eggs onto the pizza. Season with salt and pepper. Bake for 12-15 minutes or until the eggs are set and the crust is golden. Garnish with fresh basil and serve immediately.

**Raspberry Almond Danish**

**Ingredients:**

- 1 sheet puff pastry, thawed
- ¼ cup raspberry jam or fresh raspberries
- ¼ cup almond paste
- 1 egg, beaten (for egg wash)
- ¼ cup sliced almonds
- Powdered sugar (optional)

**Instructions:**

Preheat the oven to 375°F (190°C). Roll out the puff pastry and cut into squares or rectangles. Place a small amount of raspberry jam and almond paste in the center of each square. Fold the corners of the pastry to meet in the center, creating a pocket. Brush with the beaten egg, and sprinkle sliced almonds on top. Bake for 15-20 minutes or until golden and puffed. Once cooled, dust with powdered sugar if desired.

# Ham and Cheese Breakfast Casserole

**Ingredients:**

- 6 large eggs
- 1 ½ cups milk
- 2 cups cubed bread (preferably stale)
- 1 cup cooked ham, diced
- 1 cup shredded cheese (cheddar or your choice)
- ½ cup onion, diced
- 1 teaspoon mustard (optional)
- Salt and pepper, to taste

**Instructions:**

Preheat the oven to 350°F (175°C). Grease a baking dish. In a large bowl, whisk eggs, milk, mustard (if using), salt, and pepper. Layer cubed bread, ham, cheese, and onion in the baking dish. Pour the egg mixture over the top, pressing down lightly to ensure the bread absorbs the liquid. Bake for 30-35 minutes or until the eggs are set and the top is golden. Let cool slightly before slicing and serving.

**Chocolate Chip Banana Bread**

**Ingredients:**

- 2 ripe bananas, mashed
- 1 ½ cups all-purpose flour
- 1 teaspoon baking soda
- ¼ teaspoon salt
- 1/2 cup unsalted butter, softened
- ¾ cup brown sugar
- 2 large eggs
- 1 teaspoon vanilla extract
- 1 cup chocolate chips
- ½ cup sour cream or yogurt (for added moisture)

**Instructions:**

Preheat the oven to 350°F (175°C). In a bowl, whisk together the flour, baking soda, and salt. In another bowl, beat together the butter, sugar, eggs, and vanilla until smooth. Add the mashed bananas and sour cream, mixing until combined. Gradually add the dry ingredients to the wet mixture. Stir in the chocolate chips. Pour the batter into a greased loaf pan and bake for 60-70 minutes, or until a toothpick inserted comes out clean. Let cool before slicing.

**Savory Crepes with Spinach**

**Ingredients:**

- For the crepes:
    - 1 cup all-purpose flour
    - 2 large eggs
    - 1 cup milk
    - 2 tablespoons melted butter
    - A pinch of salt
- For the filling:
    - 1 cup fresh spinach, sautéed
    - ½ cup ricotta cheese
    - 1 tablespoon Parmesan cheese, grated
    - Salt and pepper, to taste

**Instructions:**

To make the crepes, whisk together flour, eggs, milk, melted butter, and salt until smooth. Heat a non-stick skillet over medium heat and lightly grease it. Pour a small amount of batter into the pan, tilting to spread it evenly. Cook for 1-2 minutes on each side, then set aside. For the filling, combine the sautéed spinach, ricotta cheese, Parmesan, salt, and pepper. Place a spoonful of the spinach mixture onto each crepe and fold or roll it up. Serve immediately.

## Maple Bacon Donuts

**Ingredients:**

- 1 ¾ cups all-purpose flour
- ½ cup sugar
- 1 teaspoon baking powder
- ¼ teaspoon salt
- ½ teaspoon cinnamon
- 2 large eggs
- ½ cup milk
- ¼ cup melted butter
- 1 teaspoon vanilla extract
- ½ cup cooked bacon, crumbled
- 1/3 cup maple syrup (for glaze)

**Instructions:**

Preheat the oven to 350°F (175°C) and grease a donut pan. In a bowl, whisk together flour, sugar, baking powder, salt, and cinnamon. In another bowl, beat eggs, milk, melted butter, and vanilla until smooth. Combine the wet and dry ingredients, then gently fold in the crumbled bacon. Spoon the batter into the donut pan and bake for 12-15 minutes or until golden. While the donuts are cooling, whisk together maple syrup and a little powdered sugar to make the glaze. Drizzle over the donuts and serve.

**Acai Smoothie Bowl**

**Ingredients:**

- 1 packet frozen acai puree
- 1 frozen banana
- ½ cup almond milk (or any milk of choice)
- ½ cup Greek yogurt (optional)
- Toppings: granola, fresh berries, chia seeds, shredded coconut

**Instructions:**

Blend the acai puree, frozen banana, almond milk, and Greek yogurt (if using) until smooth. Pour the mixture into a bowl and top with granola, fresh berries, chia seeds, and shredded coconut. Serve immediately.

**Cottage Cheese with Fresh Fruit**

**Ingredients:**

- 1 cup cottage cheese
- ½ cup mixed fresh fruit (berries, sliced peaches, pineapple, etc.)
- 1 tablespoon honey or maple syrup (optional)
- A sprinkle of cinnamon (optional)

**Instructions:**

Scoop the cottage cheese into a bowl and top with fresh fruit. Drizzle with honey or maple syrup, and sprinkle with cinnamon if desired. Serve immediately.

**Breakfast Sausage and Egg Muffins**

**Ingredients:**

- 6 eggs
- 1 cup cooked breakfast sausage, crumbled
- 1/4 cup shredded cheese (cheddar, mozzarella, or your choice)
- 1/4 cup milk
- Salt and pepper, to taste
- 1 tablespoon chopped chives (optional)

**Instructions:**

Preheat the oven to 350°F (175°C). Grease a muffin tin. In a bowl, whisk together the eggs, milk, salt, and pepper. Stir in the crumbled sausage, cheese, and chives. Pour the egg mixture into the muffin tin, filling each cup about 2/3 full. Bake for 18-20 minutes, or until the eggs are set. Let cool slightly before removing from the tin and serving.

## Tropical Fruit Salad

**Ingredients:**

- 1 cup pineapple, diced
- 1 cup mango, diced
- 1 cup papaya, diced
- 1/2 cup kiwi, sliced
- 1/2 cup coconut flakes
- Juice of 1 lime
- 1 tablespoon honey (optional)

**Instructions:**

In a large bowl, combine the pineapple, mango, papaya, kiwi, and coconut flakes. Drizzle with lime juice and honey if desired. Toss gently and serve immediately.

## Pumpkin Spice Waffles

**Ingredients:**

- 1 ½ cups all-purpose flour
- 1 teaspoon baking powder
- ½ teaspoon baking soda
- 1 teaspoon cinnamon
- ½ teaspoon nutmeg
- 1/4 teaspoon ginger
- 1/4 teaspoon salt
- 1 cup canned pumpkin puree
- 2 large eggs
- ½ cup milk
- 1 teaspoon vanilla extract
- 2 tablespoons melted butter

**Instructions:**

Preheat your waffle iron. In a bowl, whisk together the dry ingredients: flour, baking powder, baking soda, cinnamon, nutmeg, ginger, and salt. In another bowl, whisk together the pumpkin puree, eggs, milk, vanilla extract, and melted butter. Add the wet ingredients to the dry ingredients and stir until just combined. Cook the batter in the waffle iron according to the manufacturer's instructions. Serve with maple syrup or whipped cream.

**Zucchini Bread**

**Ingredients:**

- 2 cups all-purpose flour
- 1 ½ teaspoons baking powder
- 1 teaspoon baking soda
- 1 teaspoon ground cinnamon
- ¼ teaspoon salt
- 2 large eggs
- 1 cup granulated sugar
- 1 cup grated zucchini (excess moisture squeezed out)
- ½ cup vegetable oil
- 1 teaspoon vanilla extract
- 1/2 cup chopped walnuts or raisins (optional)

**Instructions:**

Preheat the oven to 350°F (175°C). Grease and flour a loaf pan. In a bowl, whisk together the flour, baking powder, baking soda, cinnamon, and salt. In another bowl, beat the eggs and sugar until smooth. Stir in the zucchini, oil, and vanilla extract. Gradually add the dry ingredients to the wet mixture, mixing until just combined. Fold in walnuts or raisins if desired. Pour the batter into the prepared loaf pan and bake for 60-70 minutes, or until a toothpick inserted comes out clean. Let cool before slicing.

**Breakfast Nachos**

**Ingredients:**

- 2 cups tortilla chips
- 2 scrambled eggs
- 1/2 cup cooked bacon or sausage, crumbled
- 1/2 cup shredded cheddar cheese
- 1/4 cup diced tomatoes
- 1/4 cup sliced jalapeños (optional)
- 1/4 cup guacamole
- 2 tablespoons sour cream
- Fresh cilantro, for garnish

**Instructions:**

Preheat your oven to 350°F (175°C). Arrange the tortilla chips in a single layer on a baking sheet. Top with scrambled eggs, bacon or sausage, and shredded cheese. Bake for 5-7 minutes, until the cheese is melted. Remove from the oven and top with diced tomatoes, jalapeños (if using), guacamole, sour cream, and cilantro. Serve immediately.

## Mango and Coconut Chia Pudding

**Ingredients:**

- 1/2 cup chia seeds
- 1 cup coconut milk (or any milk of choice)
- 1 tablespoon maple syrup or honey
- 1/2 teaspoon vanilla extract
- 1 ripe mango, peeled and diced
- Shredded coconut, for topping

**Instructions:**

In a bowl, combine the chia seeds, coconut milk, maple syrup or honey, and vanilla extract. Stir well and refrigerate for at least 4 hours or overnight to let the chia seeds absorb the liquid and thicken. Before serving, top with diced mango and shredded coconut. Enjoy!

**Baked Oatmeal Bars**

**Ingredients:**

- 2 cups rolled oats
- 1/2 cup almond milk (or any milk of choice)
- 1/4 cup honey or maple syrup
- 1/2 cup mashed bananas
- 1 teaspoon vanilla extract
- 1/2 teaspoon cinnamon
- 1/4 teaspoon salt
- 1/2 cup chopped nuts (optional)
- 1/4 cup dried fruit (raisins, cranberries, etc., optional)

**Instructions:**

Preheat the oven to 350°F (175°C) and grease a baking dish. In a large bowl, combine the oats, milk, honey or maple syrup, mashed bananas, vanilla extract, cinnamon, and salt. Stir in the nuts and dried fruit if using. Pour the mixture into the prepared baking dish and spread evenly. Bake for 25-30 minutes, until golden and set. Allow to cool before cutting into bars. Serve as a grab-and-go breakfast.

**Strawberry Yogurt Popsicles**

**Ingredients:**

- 2 cups fresh strawberries, hulled
- 1 cup plain Greek yogurt
- 1/4 cup honey or maple syrup
- 1/2 teaspoon vanilla extract

**Instructions:**

In a blender, combine the strawberries, Greek yogurt, honey or maple syrup, and vanilla extract. Blend until smooth. Pour the mixture into popsicle molds and freeze for 4-6 hours, or until fully set. To release the popsicles, run warm water over the outside of the molds. Serve as a refreshing breakfast or snack.

**Breakfast Quesadilla**

**Ingredients:**

- 2 flour tortillas
- 2 scrambled eggs
- 1/2 cup shredded cheese (cheddar or your choice)
- 1/4 cup cooked bacon or sausage, crumbled
- 1/4 cup diced bell peppers (optional)
- 1 tablespoon salsa (optional)
- Sour cream, for serving

**Instructions:**

Heat a non-stick skillet over medium heat. Place one tortilla in the skillet, then top with scrambled eggs, cheese, bacon or sausage, and bell peppers (if using). Place the second tortilla on top and cook for 2-3 minutes on each side, until golden and crispy. Remove from the skillet, slice into wedges, and serve with salsa and sour cream.

## Sourdough Toast with Ricotta and Berries

**Ingredients:**

- 2 slices sourdough bread
- 1/2 cup ricotta cheese
- 1/4 teaspoon honey or maple syrup
- 1/2 cup mixed fresh berries (strawberries, blueberries, raspberries)
- A drizzle of honey (optional)

**Instructions:**

Toast the sourdough bread slices until golden and crispy. Spread ricotta cheese on top of each slice and drizzle with honey or maple syrup. Top with mixed fresh berries and another drizzle of honey if desired. Serve immediately for a quick and delicious breakfast.

# Almond Butter and Jelly Overnight Oats

**Ingredients:**

- 1/2 cup rolled oats
- 1/2 cup almond milk (or any milk of choice)
- 2 tablespoons almond butter
- 2 tablespoons fruit preserves or jam (your choice of flavor)
- 1/2 teaspoon chia seeds (optional)

**Instructions:**

In a jar or airtight container, combine the oats, almond milk, almond butter, fruit preserves, and chia seeds (if using). Stir to combine and refrigerate overnight. In the morning, give it a quick stir and enjoy as a creamy, nutty breakfast.

## Pear and Walnut Muffins

**Ingredients:**

- 1 ½ cups all-purpose flour
- 1 teaspoon baking powder
- 1/2 teaspoon baking soda
- 1 teaspoon cinnamon
- 1/4 teaspoon salt
- 2 ripe pears, peeled and diced
- 1/2 cup chopped walnuts
- 2 large eggs
- 1/4 cup honey or maple syrup
- 1/2 cup milk
- 1/4 cup vegetable oil

**Instructions:**

Preheat the oven to 350°F (175°C) and grease a muffin tin. In a bowl, whisk together the flour, baking powder, baking soda, cinnamon, and salt. In another bowl, mix together the eggs, honey or maple syrup, milk, and oil. Add the wet ingredients to the dry ingredients and stir until just combined. Gently fold in the diced pears and chopped walnuts. Spoon the batter into the muffin tin and bake for 18-20 minutes, or until a toothpick inserted comes out clean. Allow to cool before serving.

## Classic Breakfast Sandwich

**Ingredients:**

- 2 slices whole wheat or white bread
- 1 large egg
- 1 slice cheese (cheddar, American, or your choice)
- 2 slices cooked bacon or sausage patty
- 1 tablespoon mayonnaise or mustard (optional)
- 1 leaf lettuce or tomato slice (optional)

**Instructions:**

Toast the bread slices until golden. In a skillet, cook the egg to your desired level (fried, scrambled, or poached). Place one slice of cheese on top of the egg to melt slightly. Assemble the sandwich by spreading mayonnaise or mustard on the bread, then layering the egg, bacon or sausage, and optional lettuce or tomato. Top with the other slice of toast and serve immediately.

www.ingramcontent.com/pod-product-compliance
Lightning Source LLC
LaVergne TN
LVHW081508060526
838201LV00056BA/3001